A FAIRY'S
Baking Recipes
book

LINDA BLACKMOOR

ISBN: 978-1-966417-09-5 (PRINT)

PUBLISHED BY QUILL PRESS. LINDA BLACKMOOR'S TITLES MAY BE
PURCHASED IN BULK FOR EDUCATIONAL, BUSINESS, FUNDRAISING, OR
SALES PROMOTIONAL USE. FOR INFORMATION, PLEASE EMAIL
HELLO@LINDABLACKMOOR.COM

FIRST PRINT EDITION: 2024

LINDA BLACKMOOR
WWW.LINDABLACKMOOR.COM

Ooey-Gooey Magical Chocolate Chip Cookies

INGREDIENTS:

- 2 1/4 cups all-purpose flour
- 1 teaspoon baking soda
- 1/2 teaspoon salt
- 1 cup unsalted butter, melted
- 1 cup brown sugar, packed
- 1/2 cup granulated sugar
- 2 teaspoons vanilla extract
- 2 large eggs
- 2 cups semi-sweet chocolate chips

BAKING TIME:

- Preparation: 15 minutes
- Baking: 10-12 minutes per batch
- Cooling: 5 minutes

INSTRUCTIONS:

- Set your oven to a toasty 350°F (175°C).
- In a large enchanted bowl, mix together 2 1/4 cups of flour, 1 teaspoon of baking soda, and a sprinkle of salt.
- In another bowl, blend 1 cup of melted golden butter with 1 cup of brown sugar and 1/2 cup of white sugar until they become one.
- Crack in two large eggs one at a time, stirring their magic into the mixture. Add 2 teaspoons of vanilla for that extra touch of enchantment.
- Slowly combine your dry mix with the wet magic mixture, stirring gently.
- Fold in 2 cups of chocolate chip gems, making sure they spread their sweetness throughout.
- Scoop out little balls of dough and place them on a parchment-lined baking sheet, giving them space to spread their wings.
- Place the sheet in the oven and bake for 10-12 minutes, until the edges are golden and the centers are still soft.
- Let the cookies rest on the baking sheet for 5 minutes before moving them to a wire rack to cool completely.

A Winter's Eve Crumble Apple Pie

INGREDIENTS:

- 6 cups thinly sliced, peeled apples
- 1 1/4 cup granulated sugar
- 1 cup and 2 tablespoons all-purpose flour
- 1 teaspoon ground cinnamon
- 1/4 teaspoon ground nutmeg
- 1 tablespoon lemon juice
- 1 unbaked 9-inch pie crust
- 1/2 cup packed brown sugar
- 1/2 cup unsalted butter, softened

BAKING TIME:

- Preparation: 30 minutes
- Baking: 45-50 minutes
- Cooling: 2 hours

INSTRUCTIONS:

- Wake your oven and set it to a warm 375°F.
- In a large, magical bowl, mix together 6 cups of apple slices, 3/4 cup of sugar, 2 tablespoons of flour, 1 teaspoon of cinnamon spice, 1/4 teaspoon of nutmeg, and a splash of lemon juice. Toss your mix.
- Place your unbaked pie crust in a 9-inch pie dish. Pour the apple mixture into the crust, spreading it evenly with a gentle touch.
- In a medium bowl, blend 1 cup of flour, 1/2 cup of sugar, 1/2 cup of brown sugar, and 1/2 cup of softened butter. Use a fork or your fingers to mix until the mixture resembles coarse crumbs.
- Sprinkle the crumble mixture evenly over the apples, creating a magical crust.
- Place the pie on a baking sheet to catch any drips, and bake in the preheated oven for 45-50 minutes, or until the topping is golden brown and the apples are tender.
- Allow the pie to cool on a wire rack for at least 2 hours, letting the flavors meld and the magic settle.
- Serve your apple pie with a scoop of vanilla ice cream or a dollop of whipped cream.

Sprinkled in Fairy Dust Donut Holes

INGREDIENTS:

- 1 ¼ cups all-purpose flour
- ¼ cup granulated sugar
- 1 ½ teaspoons baking powder
- ¼ teaspoon salt
- ¼ teaspoon ground nutmeg
- 1 large egg, lightly beaten
- ½ cup milk
- 1 teaspoon vanilla extract
- 2 tablespoons unsalted butter, melted and slightly cooled
- Vegetable oil
- 1 cup powdered sugar

FRYING TIME:

- Preparation: 20 minutes
- Frying: About 3-4 minutes per batch
- Cooling: 10 minutes

INSTRUCTIONS:

- In a medium mixing bowl, whisk together 1 ¼ cups of flour, ¼ cup of sugar, 1 ½ teaspoons of baking powder, ¼ teaspoon of salt, and a dash of nutmeg if desired.
- In a separate, smaller bowl, whisk together the lightly beaten egg, ½ cup of milk, 1 teaspoon of vanilla extract, and 2 tablespoons of melted butter. Gently pour the wet mixture into the dry, stirring just until a soft, sticky dough forms. Don't overmix.
- Prepare your cooking cauldron! Fill it with about 2 inches of vegetable oil and heat it to a shimmering 350°F. Be patient, as the oil must be warm.
- Once your oil is ready, use a small cookie scoop or spoon to carefully drop tablespoons of dough into the hot oil. Fry a few at a time, allowing them to gently puff and turn golden-brown, about 1-2 minutes per side. Flip them once or twice so they cook evenly.
- With a slotted spoon, lift your donut holes out of the oil and place them on a paper-towel-lined plate to drain away any excess oil. Let them rest for a few minutes, but still remain warm.
- Roll each donut hole in a bowl of powdered sugar, coating them generously. Enjoy while warm!

Over the Rainbow Fairy Cake Cups

INGREDIENTS:

- 1 ½ cups all-purpose flour
- 1 ½ teaspoons baking powder
- ¼ teaspoon salt
- ½ cup unsalted butter, softened
- 1 cup granulated sugar
- 2 large eggs, room temperature
- 1 teaspoon pure vanilla extract
- ½ cup milk, room temperature
- Gel Food Coloring, Multiple Colors
- Vanilla frosting
- Colorful sprinkles

BAKING TIME:

- Preparation: 30 minutes
- Baking: 18-20 minutes
- Cooling: 30 minutes

INSTRUCTIONS:

- Wake your oven and set it to a friendly 350°F. Line a standard 12-cup muffin tin with bright, cupcake liners.
- In a medium bowl, whisk together the flour, baking powder, and salt.
- In a larger bowl, cream the softened butter and sugar until fluffy. Add the eggs one at a time, beating well after each addition, and then stir in the vanilla extract.
- Add half of the dry mixture to the butter mixture, stirring until combined. Mix in milk gently, then add the remaining dry mix. Stir until the batter is smooth.
- Scoop out equal portions of the batter into six small bowls. Add a tiny drop of gel food coloring to each bowl, creating red, orange, yellow, green, blue, and purple batters. Stir gently until each hue is vibrant.
- Into each cupcake liner, spoon a small layer of red batter, followed by orange, yellow, green, blue, and purple. Fill each cupcake liner about ¾ full.
- Place the cupcakes into your oven and bake for 18-20 minutes, or until a toothpick inserted into the center of a cupcake emerges clean. Remove and let cupcakes rest.
- Once cooled, swirl on a dollop of vanilla frosting, like a fluffy cloud. Then add colorful sprinkles.

Wild Spring Strawberry Fruit Tarts

INGREDIENTS:

For the Crust (Tart Shells):

- 1 ½ cups all-purpose flour
- ¼ cup granulated sugar
- ½ teaspoon salt
- ½ cup cold unsalted butter, cubed
- 1 large egg yolk
- 1-2 tablespoons ice water (as needed)

For the Filling:

- 1 cup chilled pastry cream
- 1-2 cups fresh strawberries, sliced

BAKING TIME:

- Preparation: 45 minutes
- Chilling: 30 minutes (for dough)
- Baking: 15-20 minutes
- Cooling: 30 minutes

INSTRUCTIONS:

- Preheat your oven to a toasty 375°F. Ready your tart pans—six mini tart pans or one 9-inch tart pan.
- In a large bowl, whisk together the flour, sugar, and salt. Add the cold butter cubes and blend the mixture
- Add the egg yolk and stir gently. Shape the dough into a disc, wrap it in plastic, and let it rest in the refrigerator for 30 minutes.
- On a lightly floured surface, roll out the chilled dough to about ¼-inch thickness. Press it into your tart pan(s), trimming the edges. Prick the bottom of the crust with a fork a few times to prevent puffing.
- Place a piece of foil inside each crust and fill with pie weights, dried beans, or rice. Bake for 12 minutes, then remove the weights and bake for an additional 3-5 minutes, until the edges turn lightly golden.
- Remove the tart shells from the oven and let them rest on a wire rack until completely cool. Then spoon the chilled pastry cream into the shells.
- Arrange your strawberries atop the pastry cream in a pattern, like a rose. Then enjoy!

Dark Forest
Enchanted Brownies

INGREDIENTS:

- 1 cup (2 sticks) unsalted butter, melted and cooled slightly
- 2 cups granulated sugar
- 4 large eggs, room temperature
- 1 teaspoon pure vanilla extract
- ¾ cup unsweetened cocoa powder
- 1 cup all-purpose flour
- ¼ teaspoon salt
- 1 cup chocolate chips or chunks

BAKING TIME:

- Preparation: 20 minutes
- Baking: 25-30 minutes
- Cooling: 30 minutes

INSTRUCTIONS:

- Begin by preheating your oven to 350°F. Line an 8x8-inch baking pan with parchment paper, letting it drape over the edges—this helps lift the brownies out later.
- In a large bowl, stir together the melted butter and sugar. Add in the eggs one by one then pour in the vanilla extract. Stir until the mixture is smooth.
- Sift in the cocoa powder, flour, and salt. Stir gently with a wooden spoon or spatula until just combined— imagine you're blending secret spells into the batter. If you choose, fold in a handful of chocolate chips or chunks for extra bursts of enchanted sweetness.
- Pour the batter into your prepared pan, using a spatula to smooth it into an even, chocolatey blanket. Give the pan a little wiggle to settle any mischievous air bubbles.
- Place the pan in the oven and bake for 25-30 minutes. The brownies are done when a toothpick inserted near the center comes out with just a few moist crumbs.
- Remove the brownies from the oven and let them rest on a wire rack for about 30 minutes. This ensures each bite is chewy, fudgy, and just a bit magical. Enjoy with a glass of milk!

Golden Morning Dew Banana Muffins

INGREDIENTS:

- 1 ½ cups all-purpose flour
- 1 teaspoon baking soda
- ½ teaspoon baking powder
- ½ teaspoon ground cinnamon
- ¼ teaspoon salt
- 3 very ripe bananas, mashed
- ½ cup granulated sugar
- 1 large egg, lightly beaten
- ⅓ cup unsalted butter, melted
- 1 teaspoon pure vanilla extract

BAKING TIME:

- Preparation: 20 minutes
- Baking: 20-25 minutes
- Cooling: 10 minutes

INSTRUCTIONS:

- Preheat your oven to 375°F and line a 12-cup muffin tin with paper liners.
- In a medium bowl, whisk together the flour, baking soda, baking powder, cinnamon, and salt.
- In a larger bowl, stir together the mashed bananas, sugar, beaten egg, melted butter, and vanilla extract. The batter will smell like a sunny morning in a secret fairy garden—sweet and comforting.
- Gently fold the dry mixture into the banana mixture, stirring just until combined. Don't overmix.
- Scoop the batter into the prepared muffin cups, filling them about ¾ full. Don't worry if the tops look a bit bumpy—the muffins will bloom into golden treats.
- Place the tin in the preheated oven and bake for 20-25 minutes, or until a toothpick inserted into a muffin comes out with just a crumb or two.
- Let the muffins rest in the tin for a few minutes before transferring them to a wire rack to cool. Serve them warm with a little butter or honey and enjoy!

The Fairy Queen's Sugar Cookies

INGREDIENTS:

- 2 ¾ cups all-purpose flour
- 1 teaspoon baking soda
- ½ teaspoon baking powder
- 1 cup (2 sticks) unsalted butter, softened
- 1 ½ cups granulated sugar
- 1 large egg
- 1 teaspoon vanilla extract
- ½ teaspoon almond extract
- 3 tablespoons milk
- Sprinkles, colored sugars, or edible glitter

BAKING TIME:

- Preparation: 20 minutes
- Baking: 8-10 minutes per batch
- Cooling: 10 minutes

INSTRUCTIONS:

- Set your oven to a warm 375°F. Line baking sheets with parchment paper or silicone mats.
- In a medium bowl, whisk together the all-purpose flour, baking soda, and baking powder.
- In a large mixing bowl, use an electric mixer to cream together the softened butter and granulated sugar.
- Beat in the egg, vanilla extract, and almond extract (if using) to the butter-sugar mixture. Pour in the milk and continue to mix until everything is smooth.
- Gradually add the dry ingredient mixture to the wet ingredients, mix on low until the dough comes together.
- Scoop out tablespoon-sized portions of dough and roll them into balls. Place them onto the prepared baking sheets, spacing them about 2 inches apart. Gently press each ball down with your palm to flatten slightly.
- Sprinkle your cookies with colorful sprinkles.
- Bake for 8-10 minutes, or until the edges are just beginning to turn golden. These treats bake quickly!
- Remove the cookies from the oven and let them cool for about 5 -10 minutes before enjoying a warm treat!

Cinnamon Whirl Snickerdoodle Swirls

INGREDIENTS:

- 2¾ cups all-purpose flour
- 1½ teaspoons cream of tartar
- 1 teaspoon baking soda
- ½ teaspoon salt
- 1 cup (2 sticks) unsalted butter, softened
- 1½ cups granulated sugar
- 2 large eggs
- 1 teaspoon pure vanilla extract

For Rolling:

- 3 tablespoons granulated sugar
- 1½ teaspoons ground cinnamon

BAKING TIME:

- Preparation: 20 minutes
- Baking: 8–10 minutes per batch
- Cooling: 5–10 minutes

INSTRUCTIONS:

- Preheat your oven to 375°F. Line your baking sheets with parchment paper.
- In a medium bowl, whisk together the flour, cream of tartar, baking soda, and salt.
- In a large bowl, use an electric mixer to cream the softened butter and sugar. Beat in the eggs one by one, then stir in the vanilla.
- Gradually add the flour mixture to the butter-sugar mixture, blending slow until a soft cookie dough forms.
- In a small dish, combine the extra sugar and cinnamon. Scoop tablespoon-sized portions of dough, roll them into balls, then roll each in the cinnamon-sugar mix.
- Place the cinnamon-sugar-coated dough balls onto the prepared baking sheets, leaving a couple of inches between them so they have room to puff.
- Bake for 8–10 minutes. Keep watch—the edges should just begin to turn golden while the centers remain soft.
- Remove the cookies from the oven and let them rest on the baking sheets for a few minutes before transferring them to a wire rack. Let them cool fully before enjoying this cinnamon delight.

Woodland Harvest Oatmeal Raisin Cookies

INGREDIENTS:

- 1 cup (2 sticks) unsalted butter, softened
- 1 cup packed brown sugar
- ½ cup granulated sugar
- 2 large eggs, room temperature
- 1 teaspoon pure vanilla extract
- 1¾ cups all-purpose flour
- 1 teaspoon baking soda
- ½ teaspoon salt
- 1 teaspoon ground cinnamon
- 2 cups old-fashioned rolled oats
- 1 cup raisins
- 1 cup chocolate chips

BAKING TIME:

- Preparation: 20 minutes
- Baking: 10–12 minutes per batch
- Cooling: 5–10 minutes

INSTRUCTIONS:

- Preheat your oven to 350°F. Line your baking sheets with parchment paper.
- In a large mixing bowl, cream the softened butter, brown sugar, and granulated sugar until light and fluffy. Beat in the eggs one at a time, followed by the vanilla extract, blending until everything is smooth.
- In a separate bowl, whisk together the flour, baking soda, salt, and cinnamon. Add this dry mixture to the butter-sugar mixture and stir gently until combined.
- Fold in the old-fashioned oats, raisins, and chocolate chips.
- Drop rounded tablespoons of dough onto the prepared baking sheets, leaving a bit of space so they can spread.
- Bake for 10–12 minutes, or until the edges are golden and the centers still appear slightly soft.
- Remove the cookies from the oven and let them rest for a few minutes on the baking sheets before transferring them to a wire rack.
- Serve your delicious cookies alongside a glass of milk or a cup of tea. Enjoy!

Magical Meadow Krispie Marshmallow Bars

INGREDIENTS:

- 3 tablespoons unsalted butter
- 1 (10 oz) package marshmallows (mini or regular)
- 6 cups crispy rice cereal
- A sprinkle of colorful candy sprinkles or M&Ms.

PREP TIME:

- Preparation: 15 minutes
- Cooling: 30 minutes

INSTRUCTIONS:

- In a large, sturdy pot, melt the butter over low heat. Add the marshmallows and stir patiently as they soften and become velvety—like a fluffy cloud.
- Once the marshmallows have fully melted, remove the pot from the heat and gently fold in the crispy rice cereal. Stir until every grain is coated.
- Lightly butter a 9x13-inch baking dish, then spoon the gooey mixture inside. With a sheet of parchment paper or lightly buttered hands, press it down firmly until it forms a smooth, even layer. If you'd like, scatter some colorful candy sprinkles on top or mix in some M&M candies or other preferred candies.
- Let the bars rest at room temperature for about 30 minutes, allowing them to set.
- Cut the set mixture into squares and serve. Enjoy this easy yet magical treat! The fairies love gifting these to the pixies.

Elf King's Peanut Butter Cookies

INGREDIENTS:

- 1 cup creamy peanut butter
- ½ cup (1 stick) unsalted butter, softened
- ½ cup granulated sugar
- ½ cup packed brown sugar
- 1 large egg, room temperature
- 1 teaspoon pure vanilla extract
- 1½ cups all-purpose flour
- 1 teaspoon baking soda
- ¼ teaspoon salt

BAKING TIME:

- Preparation: 15 minutes
- Chilling (optional): 30 minutes for puffier cookies
- Baking: 8–10 minutes per batch
- Cooling: 10 minutes

INSTRUCTIONS:

- Preheat your oven to 375°F and line your baking sheets with parchment paper.
- In a large bowl, beat together the peanut butter, softened butter, granulated sugar, and brown sugar until light and fluffy. Crack in the egg, pour in the vanilla, and mix again.
- In a separate bowl, whisk the flour, baking soda, and salt. Gently stir this dry blend into the peanut butter mixture until a soft cookie dough forms. If it feels a bit sticky and mischievous, chill it in the fridge for about 30 minutes to help it calm down.
- Scoop tablespoon-sized portions of dough and roll them into balls. Place them on your prepared baking sheets, leaving room for them to spread. Use a fork to press a crisscross pattern on top of each cookie.
- Pop the baking sheets into the oven and bake for 8–10 minutes. Keep watch—your cookies should be lightly golden at the edges but still soft in the center.
- Remove the sheets from the oven and let the cookies rest for a few minutes before transferring them to a wire rack. Enjoy your yummy creation!

A Sprinkle of Sunshine
Lemon Bars

INGREDIENTS:

Crust:

- 1 cup (2 sticks) unsalted butter, softened
- ½ cup granulated sugar
- 2 cups all-purpose flour
- ¼ teaspoon salt

Lemon Filling:

- 4 large eggs, room temperature
- 1½ cups granulated sugar
- ¼ cup all-purpose flour
- Zest of 1 lemon
- ⅔ cup freshly squeezed lemon juice
- A dusting of powdered sugar for garnish

BAKING TIME:

- Preparation: 20 minutes
- Baking: 50 minutes
- Cooling: 2 hours

INSTRUCTIONS:

- Warm your oven to 350°F. Line a 9x13-inch baking dish with parchment paper, letting the edges drape over the sides.

- In a large bowl, cream together the softened butter and sugar until fluffy. Stir in the flour and salt until a soft, crumbly dough forms. Press this mixture into the bottom of your prepared pan, patting it gently.

- Slide the pan into your oven and bake for 20–25 minutes, or until the crust turns a soft, golden hue.

- In a separate bowl, whisk together the eggs, sugar, flour, lemon zest, and lemon juice.

- Remove the crust from the oven and carefully pour the lemon filling over the hot crust. Return the pan to the oven and bake for another 20–25 minutes, or until the top is set and no longer jiggles like a giggling sprite.

- Place the pan on a wire rack and let it cool completely —about 2 hours.

- Once cooled, use the parchment cloak to lift the lemon bars from the pan. Dust the top with powdered sugar, then slice into squares. Each bite is a burst of brightness and sweet tang, like tasting a drop of sunshine. Enjoy!

Goblin's Mud Covered Chocolate Pretzels

INGREDIENTS:

- About 2 cups of pretzel twists or rods
- 8 oz high-quality chocolate (milk, dark, or white), finely chopped
- 1 tablespoon vegetable oil (if needed, to thin the chocolate)
- Colorful sprinkles, chopped nuts, or crushed toffee bits (for a whimsical crunch)

PREP TIME:

- Preparation: 20 minutes
- Setting: 30 minutes

INSTRUCTIONS:

- Begin by setting out a sheet of parchment paper on a baking sheet.
- In a microwave-safe bowl, gently melt the chopped chocolate in 20-second bursts, stirring between each, until smooth and glossy like a polished magic mirror. If the chocolate seems too thick, stir in a teaspoon or so of vegetable oil to help it flow easily.
- Dip each pretzel rod halfway into the warm chocolate (or fully cover pretzel twists), giving it a sweet, chocolaty coat. Tap off any excess chocolate, letting it drizzle back into the bowl like tiny chocolate raindrops.
- While the chocolate is still soft, sprinkle on your toppings—think colorful candy sprinkles for a rainbow shimmer or chopped nuts for a woodland crunch.
- Lay the decorated pretzels onto your parchment-lined sheet and let them rest for about 30 minutes.
- Once the chocolate has hardened and the decorations are secure, serve your chocolate-covered pretzels to friends and family. Enjoy the treat the goblins love best!

Rainbow Sunset Funfetti Cake Pops

INGREDIENTS:

- 1 box of funfetti cake mix (plus ingredients listed on the box)
- ½ cup frosting (vanilla or cream cheese)
- 12 oz candy melts or white chocolate, finely chopped
- 1 tablespoon vegetable oil (if needed to thin the chocolate)
- Colorful sprinkles (for decorating)
- Cake pop sticks

BAKING TIME

- Preparation: 45 minutes
- Cake Baking: According to box directions
- Cake Pop Chilling: 30 minutes
- Chocolate Setting: 15-20 minutes

INSTRUCTIONS:

- Prepare and bake the funfetti cake mix according to the box instructions.
- Once the cake is baked and cooled, crumble it into a large mixing bowl until it becomes fine, fluffy crumbs.
- Stir in the frosting, a little at a time, until the mixture holds together like soft, moldable clay.
- Scoop tablespoon-sized portions of the cake mixture and roll them into smooth balls. Place them on a parchment-lined baking sheet. Put them in fridge for 30 minutes to firm up.
- In a microwave-safe bowl, melt the chocolate in 20-second bursts, stirring between each round. If it seems too thick, stir in a teaspoon of vegetable oil.
- Take a cake pop stick, dip one end into the melted chocolate, and then insert it halfway into a chilled cake ball. Dip the cake pop into the melted chocolate, twirling gently to coat it fully. Drip off any excess.
- Before the chocolate sets, sprinkle each pop with extra rainbow sprinkles.
- Place the finished cake pops stick-side-up in a foam block or a sturdy cup to let the chocolate harden. After 15-20 minutes, they'll be ready to enjoy!